Stephen Fide

CHRISTIAN BIBLE TRIVIA GAME

Fun Multiple Choice Quizzes for Bible Study

— Large Print —

Bon Roi Press

Copyright © 2024 Stephen Fide.

ISBN 978-1-965785-07-2 (Paperback)

978-1-965785-08-9 (Hardcover)

Publisher: Bon Roi Press

"All scripture is given by inspiration of God, and is profitable for doctrine, for reproof, for correction, for instruction in righteousness."
2 Timothy 3:16 (KJV)

CONTENTS

Jesus..............................2

The Apostles.....................15

Sin in the Bible.................27

The Prophets.....................39

Israel...........................51

Women of the Bible...............63

God's Covenants..................75

Salvation in the Bible...........80

Biblical Places..................89

Biblical Characters..............101

The Bible........................113

How to Play

Welcome to the *Christian Bible Trivia Game!* In the following pages you will come across various quizzes on different biblical topics. These quizzes can be completed by oneself or with company. If there are multiple players, each may keep score with a separate pen and paper. The quiz questions range from easy to challenging, so get your Bibles out! Here are some fun options for playing this game with more than one person:

- Set a short timer for everyone to look up a difficult question in the Bible.
- Write every person's name on a sheet of paper or scoreboard. Keep score by using tally marks under each name.
- Form teams of two. Take turns tag-teaming to answer questions.

Now let the games begin!

JESUS

33 QUESTIONS

For where two or three are gathered together in my name, there am I in the midst of them.
Matthew 18:20

1. Who was Jesus' earthly father?

A) James

B) Joseph

C) Joshua

D) Josiah

2. In which city was Jesus born? In which other city did He grow up?

A) Nazareth and Jerusalem

B) Jerusalem and Bethlehem

C) Bethlehem and Nazareth

D) Nazareth and Bethlehem

3. Jesus said, "You cannot serve God and _____."

A) hate.

B) man.

C) Baal.

D) mannon.

4. *What did God say during Jesus' baptism?*

A) "He is my beloved Son"

B) "Repent and be saved"

C) "Go forth and preach"

D) "You are blessed"

5. *Who baptized Jesus?*

A) Peter

B) James

C) John the Baptist

D) Paul

6. *How many parables did Jesus teach?*

A) Over 20

B) Over 80

C) Over 10

D) Over 40

7. Where did Jesus walk on water?

A) Sea of Galilee

B) Dead Sea

C) Jordan River

D) Red Sea

8. What was Jesus' ethnicity?

A) Sumerian

B) Jewish

C) Egyptian

D) Persian

9. Before Jesus started preaching, what was his occupation?

A) Shepherd

B) Fisherman

C) Carpenter

D) Priest

10. How many disciples did Jesus choose?

A) 10

B) 11

C) 12

D) 13

11. What is another one of Jesus' names?

A) Enoch

B) Josiah

C) Hebron

D) Immanuel

12. Why did Jesus weep in John 11:35?

A) He was hungry for he was starving

B) He was saddened by someone's death

C) He was hurt due to betrayal

D) He was pained, injured by an enemy

13. Which disciple denied Jesus three times?

A) Peter

B) John

C) Andrew

D) James

14. What happened after Jesus was buried in the tomb?

A) He disappeared.

B) He rose again.

C) He was moved to a new tomb.

D) The tomb was destroyed.

15. On what day of the week did Jesus rise from the dead?

A) Friday

B) Saturday

C) Sunday

D) Monday

16. Where was Jesus born?

A) In an inn.

B) In a manger.

C) In a barn.

D) In a field.

17. Who anointed Jesus' feet with expensive perfume?

A) Mary Magdalene

B) Martha

C) Elizabeth

D) Joanna

18. What did Jesus use to feed the 5,000?

A) Bread and wine

B) Bread and fish

C) Fish and olives

D) Bread and honey

19. How old was Jesus when His parents couldn't find Him for three days?

A) 13

B) 9

C) 12

D) 10

20. What happened before Jesus started His preaching?

A) A neighbor helped Him.

B) The devil failed to tempt Him.

C) He got lost in a temple.

D) Peter made a pact with Him.

21. Jesus said "You must be born again" to

A) Peter.

B) John.

C) Nicodemus.

D) Lazarus.

22. Jesus passed away on the cross at:

A) the sixth hour.

B) the ninth hour.

C) the fourth hour.

D) the seventh hour.

23. What did Jesus say to the storm while on a boat with His disciples?

A) "Be quiet!"

B) "Go away!"

C) "Be still!"

D) "Peace, be calm!"

24. Which Old Testament figure was related to Jesus by blood?

A) King David

B) Prophet Isaiah

C) Prophet Joshua

D) King Saul

25. From where did Jesus ascend into heaven?

A) Mount Sinai

B) Mount Olives

C) Mount Carmel

D) Mount Zion

26. For how many days did Jesus appear to people after His resurrection?

A) 7 days

B) 12 days

C) 30 days

D) 40 days

27. Who first saw Jesus after His resurrection?

A) Mary Magdalene

B) Peter

C) Mary of Cleophas

D) Thomas

28. Under whose orders was Jesus crucified?

A) Emperor Tiberius

B) High Priest Tacitus

C) Governor Pilate

D) Emperor Augustus

29. Who helped carry Jesus' cross?

A) Peter

B) Simon of Cyrene

C) John

D) Joseph of Arimathea

30. What was placed on Jesus' head during the crucifixion?

A) A crown of thorns

B) A crown of coal

C) A crown of gold

D) A crown of the star of David

31. How did Jesus enter Jerusalem before his crucifixion?

A) On a horse

B) On a donkey

C) On a chariot

D) On foot

32. What did Jesus do right after His Sermon on the Mount?

A) He turned water into wine.

B) He healed someone with leprosy.

C) He spoke to a prostitute at a well.

D) He spoke with Satan.

33. Which disciple betrayed Jesus?

A) Peter

B) Judas Iscariot

C) John

D) Thomas

ANSWERS

1. B)	2. C)	3. D)
4. A)	5. C)	6. D)
7. A)	8. B)	9. C)
10. C)	11. D)	12. B)
13. A)	14. B)	15. C)
16. B)	17. A)	18. B)
19. C)	20. B)	21. C)
22. B)	23. C)	24. A)
25. B)	26. D)	27. A)
28. C)	29. B)	30. A)
31. B)	32. B)	33. B)

...And we have a winner!

THE APOSTLES

30 QUESTIONS

And he said unto them, Go ye into all the world, and preach the gospel to every creature.

Mark 16:15

34. Who was the apostle known for doubting Jesus' resurrection?

A) Peter

B) John

C) Thomas

D) James

35. Who was the leader of the apostles after Jesus' ascension?

A) John

B) Peter

C) Matthew

D) Andrew

36. What was Paul's original name?

A) Saul

B) Simon

C) Levi

D) Andrew

37. Which apostles were fishermen?

A) Matthew, John, Luke and Judas

B) Philip, James, Andrew, Saul

C) Simon, Andrew, James and John

D) Saul, Philip, James and John

38. Which apostle was called "the disciple whom Jesus loved"?

A) Peter

B) James

C) John

D) Andrew

39. Who was the first apostle to be martyred?

A) John

B) James

C) Peter

D) Thomas

40. Who replaced Judas as one of the twelve apostles?

A) Matthias

B) Paul

C) Barnabas

D) Silas

41. Who traveled extensively to spread the gospel to the Gentiles?

A) Peter

B) James

C) Paul

D) John

42. Which two apostles were brothers?

A) Peter and Andrew

B) Paul and Barnabas

C) John and Matthew

D) Judas and Matthias

43. Which apostle was present at the crucifixion of Jesus?

A) Thomas

B) Peter

C) James

D) John

44. Which apostle preached at Pentecost?

A) Paul

B) Peter

C) John

D) Andrew

45. Which apostle wrote most of the New Testament letters?

A) John

B) Peter

C) Paul

D) James

46. Which apostle took care of Jesus' mother after Jesus was crucified?

A) Philip

B) Saul

C) John

D) Mark

47. Who did Jesus praise for his honesty?

A) Peter

B) James

C) Andrew

D) Bartholomew

48. Which apostle was a former Pharisee and Roman citizen?

A) Peter

B) John

C) Paul

D) Andrew

49. Which apostle questioned Jesus, asking how they'd know the way to where He was going?

A) Thomas

B) Philip

C) John

D) Peter

50. Who was the first apostle Jesus called?

A) Peter

B) Andrew

C) James

D) John

51. Jesus gave which apostles the nickname "Sons of Thunder" due to their temper?

A) Philip and Jude

B) James and Philip

C) John and Paul

D) James and John

52. Which apostle was a philosopher?

A) James

B) Paul

C) Philip

D) Bartholomew

53. Who said, "Silver and gold I do not have, but what I do have I give you"?

A) Peter

B) Paul

C) John

D) Matthew

54. Who preached to the Ethiopian eunuch and baptized him on the road?

A) Peter

B) Philip

C) James

D) John

55. How did the cross look that Andrew the Apostle died upon?

A) It was an X.

B) It was upside-down.

C) It was severed.

D) It was smaller than normal.

56. Who was the only apostle to die of old age?

A) Peter

B) Paul

C) John

D) James

57. Which two apostles were brothers and fishermen before following Jesus?

A) James and John

B) Peter and Andrew

C) Matthew and Thomas

D) Philip and Bartholomew

58. Which apostle was known for persecuting Christians before converting to Christianity?

A) Stephen

B) Paul

C) Matthias

D) Barnabas

59. Which apostle wrote Revelation?

A) Peter

B) James

C) Paul

D) John

60. Who converted the then King of Armenia to Christianity?

A) Luke

B) Paul

C) Bartholomew

D) John

61. Who was instructed by Jesus to "tend my sheep"?

A) Peter

B) John

C) Andrew

D) Matthew

62. Who was the apostle that took the Gospel to India?

A) John

B) Thomas

C) Philip

D) James

63. Which two apostles were sons of Zebedee?

A) Peter and Andrew

B) Thomas and Matthew

C) Philip and Bartholomew

D) James and John

ANSWERS

34. C)	35. B)	36. A)
37. C)	38. C)	39. B)
40. A)	41. C)	42. A)
43. D)	44. B)	45. C)
46. C)	47. D)	48. C)
49. A)	50. B)	51. D)
52. B)	53. A)	54. B)
55. A)	56. C)	57. B)
58. B)	59. D)	60. C)
61. A)	62. C)	63. D)

Not too shabby.

SIN IN THE BIBLE

30 QUESTIONS

For all have sinned, and come short of the glory of God.
Romans 3:23

64. What are two of the seven deadly sins?

A) sloth and gluttony

B) gluttony and murder

C) drunkenness and pride

D) wrath and witchcraft

65. Who was the first person to commit murder in the Bible?

A) Adam

B) Cain

C) Abel

D) Lamech

66. According to the Bible, who is credited with introducing sin into the world?

A) Satan

B) Noah

C) Eve

D) Adam

67. What was King David's sin that led to the death of Uriah?

A) Theft

B) Murder

C) Coveting

D) Deception

68. The Bible says "the wages of sin" is

A) wealth.

B) sorrow.

C) death.

D) despair.

69. Which king was punished with leprosy for unlawfully offering incense in the temple?

A) Uzziah

B) Nebuchadnezzer

C) Solomon

D) David

70. According to the Ten Commandments, what sin is committed when someone lies?

A) Stealing

B) Giving false testimony

C) Coveting

D) Dishonoring parents

71. Why was Lucifer kicked out of Heaven?

A) Lying and boastfulness

B) Jealousy and drunkenness

C) Rebellion and Pride

D) Drunkenness and uncleanliness

72. What was the sin of Ananias and Sapphira in the Book of Acts?

A) Disobeying the apostles

B) Stealing from the temple

C) Refusing to share with the poor

D) Lying about their offering

73. What does sin mean in Hebrew?

A) To disobey

B) To harm or injure

C) To fail or to miss

D) To stop trying

74. What cleanses us from all sin?

A) Good works

B) Jesus' blood

C) Prayers

D) Fasting

75. Who was told by God, "...And if you do not do well, sin is crouching at the door"?

A) Cain

B) Abel

C) Lamech

D) Enoch

76. *According to Proverbs, what does pride lead to?*

A) Envy

B) Sadness

C) Destruction

D) Success

77. *Which commandment forbids coveting?*

A) Sixth

B) Eighth

C) Ninth

D) Tenth

78. *In the Bible, which city was destroyed because of the sins of its people?*

A) Jericho

B) Bethel

C) Ai

D) Sodom

79. Who told Eve to eat the forbidden fruit?

A) A serpent

B) Adam

C) An angel

D) A prophet

80. Which of these sins is considered the "root of all evil" in 1 Timothy?

A) Sloth

B) Pride

C) Greed

D) Lust

81. What did Cain feel that led him to kill his brother Abel?

A) Betrayal

B) Jealousy

C) Boredom

D) Humiliation

82. *According to James 4:17, what is a sin?*

A) Doing wrong

B) Being kind to others

C) Thinking negative thoughts

D) Knowing good and not doing it

83. *What did Achan take, which led to Israel's defeat at Ai?*

A) Gold and expensive food

B) A robe and fine metals

C) A large tent

D) A lamb

84. *In Romans, who does Paul say will rescue us from "this body of death" caused by sin?*

A) Moses

B) Jesus Christ

C) John the Baptist

D) Angels

85. According to Proverbs, what does "a lying tongue" do?

A) Builds trust

B) Causes chaos

C) Hates those it hurts

D) Pleases God

86. What sin was Rahab known for?

A) Prostitution

B) Gossip

C) Murder

D) Selfishness

87. Why is murder bad?

A) Because it can be bloody

B) Because we are to be fruitful

C) Because it is unexpected

D) Because man is made in God's image

88. According to Jesus, what causes a person to commit adultery in their heart?

A) Giving a gift

B) Abstinence

C) Looking with lustful intent

D) Ignoring their spouse

89. In the Book of Jonah, which city repented of its sins to avoid destruction?

A) Jericho

B) Sodom

C) Gomorrah

D) Nineveh

90. What is the unforgiveable sin?

A) Blasphemy against the Father

B) Blasphemy against the Holy Spirit

C) Murder

D) Denying Christ

91. Jesus taught you should forgive those who sin against you how many times?

A) Twice

B) Eleven and seven times

C) Seventy times seven

D) One hundred times

92. Who led Israel into idol worship?

A) Solomon

B) Jeroboam

C) Aaron

D) All of the above

93. According to the Bible, whose sin led to the fall of Jerusalem and captivity in Babylon?

A) Moses

B) Nebuchadnezzar

C) The people of Judah

D) Haman

ANSWERS

64. A)	65. B)	66. D)
67. C)	68. C)	69. A)
70. B)	71. C)	72. D)
73. C)	74. B)	75. A)
76. A)	77. C)	78. D)
79. A)	80. C)	81. B)
82. D)	83. B)	84. B)
85. C)	86. A)	87. A)
88. C)	89. D)	90. B)
91. C)	92. D)	93. C)

Smarter than Solomon.

THE PROPHETS

30 QUESTIONS

And when this cometh to pass,
(lo, it will come,) then shall
they know that a prophet hath
been among them.
Ezekiel 33:33

94. Who was swallowed by a great fish?

A) Jonah

B) Elijah

C) Amos

D) Micah

95. Who was the prophet that confronted King Ahab and Queen Jezebel?

A) Elijah

B) Isaiah

C) Hosea

D) Jeremiah

96. Which prophet saw the valley of dry bones?

A) Isaiah

B) Jeremiah

C) Ezekiel

D) Daniel

97. Who was the prophet known for interpreting dreams for Nebudchadnezzar?

A) Joel

B) Hosea

C) Daniel

D) Zechariah

98. Who warned the people of Nineveh to repent?

A) Nahum

B) Amos

C) Micah

D) Jonah

99. Which prophet was taken up to heaven in a whirlwind?

A) Jeremiah

B) Elijah

C) Amos

D) Isaiah

100. *Who is known as the "weeping prophet"?*

A) Isaiah

B) Jeremiah

C) Ezekiel

D) Hosea

101. *Which prophet married Gomer to symbolize God's relationship with Israel?*

A) Hosea

B) Joel

C) Amos

D) Micah

102. *Who prophesied the Messiah and described Him as a "suffering servant"?*

A) Ezekiel

B) Isaiah

C) Zephaniah

D) Joel

103. Who had a vision of a "wheel within a wheel"?

A) Daniel

B) Isaiah

C) Ezekiel

D) Amos

104. Which prophet prophesied against the city of Edom?

A) Obadiah

B) Jonah

C) Zephaniah

D) Habakkuk

105. Who rebuked Israel for their false sacrifices and empty rituals?

A) Joel

B) Hosea

C) Zechariah

D) Amos

106. Which prophet had a vision of 4 horsemen?

A) Zechariah

B) Micah

C) Nahum

D) Malachi

107. Who questioned God about why the wicked are allowed to prosper?

A) Habakkuk

B) Zephaniah

C) Nahum

D) Haggai

108. Which prophet's book starts with a conversation between him and God?

A) Malachi

B) Amos

C) Haggai

D) Habakkuk

109. Who was the last prophet of the Old Testament?

A) Zechariah

B) Haggai

C) Malachi

D) Micah

110. Who had a vision of a flying scroll?

A) Joel

B) Zechariah

C) Amos

D) Jonah

111. Who saw a vision of God's glory departing from the temple?

A) Jeremiah

B) Daniel

C) Amos

D) Ezekiel

112. Who was the first prophet in the Bible?

A) Abraham

B) Moses

C) Adam

D) Hosea

113. How many major prophets are in the Old testament?

A) 8

B) 4 to 5

C) 10 to 12

D) 3

114. Which prophet compared the relationship of God and Israel to a potter and clay?

A) Amos

B) Abraham

C) Jeremiah

D) Hosea

115. In Isaiah's vision, which creatures had six wings and called out "Holy, Holy, Holy"?

A) Cherubim

B) Angels with trumpets

C) Eagles

D) Seraphim

116. How did Jonah refuse God's call?

A) He built an altar.

B) He hid in a temple.

C) He made a sacrifice in the wilderness.

D) He fled to a distant city.

117. Who was the last prophet of the Old Covenant before the arrival of Jesus?

A) John the Baptist

B) Isaiah

C) Amos

D) Malachi

118. Who was the most important NT prophet?

A) John the Baptist

B) Jesus Christ

C) Paul the Apostle

D) Jeremiah

119. Who warned the people not to trust in "lying words" and empty rituals?

A) Ezekiel

B) Joshua

C) Jeremiah

D) Zechariah

120. The prophet Micah asked, "What does the Lord require of you?" What was the answer?

A) "Act justly, love kindness, walk humbly."

B) "Offer sacrifices, fast regularly, give alms."

C) "Obey without question, trust blindly."

D) "Worship daily, pray without ceasing."

121. God told which prophet to wear a yoke to symbolize Judah's slavery under Babylon?

A) Samson

B) Hosea

C) Isaiah

D) Jeremiah

122. Which prophet made fun of Baal?

A) Isaial

B) Samuel

C) Elijah

D) Ezra

123. In which book is there a prophecy of swords turned to plowshares?

A) Joshua

B) Deuteronomy

C) Nehemiah

D) Isaiah

ANSWERS

94. A)	95. A)	96. C)
97. C)	98. D)	99. B)
100. B)	101. A)	102. B)
103. C)	104. A)	105. D)
106. A)	107. A)	108. D)
109. C)	110. B)	111. D)
112. A)	113. B)	114. C)
115. D)	116. D)	117. A)
118. B)	119. C)	120. A)
121. D)	122. C)	123. D)

Good game!

ISRAEL

30 QUESTIONS

*Yet the number of the children
of Israel shall be as the sand of
the sea, which cannot be
measured nor numbered...*
Hosea 1:10

124. Who led the Israelites out of Egypt?

A) Caleb

B) Aaron

C) Joshua

D) Moses

125. What sea did the Israelites cross during the Exodus?

A) Red Sea

B) Dead Sea

C) Sea of Galilee

D) Jordan River

126. Who was the second leader of Israel?

A) Aaron

B) Caleb

C) Joshua

D) Gideon

127. *Which city's walls fell after the Israelites marched around it?*

A) Jerusalem

B) Jericho

C) Gideon

D) Aaron

128. *How many tribes made up Israel?*

A) 10

B) 12

C) 7

D) 13

129. *Who was the first king of Israel?*

A) Saul

B) David

C) Solomon

D) Samuel

130. What did the Israelites use the Ark of the Covenant for?

A) For organizing military strategies

B) For storing and preserving food

C) For storing the Ten Commandments

D) For making sacrifices to God

131. What was the Tabernacle?

A) A place of worship for the Israelites

B) An Israelite storage with divine relics

C) A rest stop for the Israelites

D) A prison for Israelite enemies

132. Who built the first temple in Jerusalem?

A) David

B) Saul

C) Rehoboam

D) Solomon

133. What was the main language spoken in ancient Israel?

A) Hebrew

B) Greek

C) Aramaic

D) Egyptian

134. Who led Israel into the Promised Land?

A) Moses

B) Joshua

C) Aaron

D) Caleb

135. Who wrestled with God and was renamed Israel?

A) Abraham

B) Isaac

C) Jacob

D) Moses

136. What food did God provide for Israel in the wilderness?

A) Fruit

B) Bread

C) Quail

D) Manna

137. Who was the judge that led Israel against the Philistines with a small army?

A) Gideon

B) Samson

C) Deborah

D) Ehud

138. Why did God tell Israel to fight Canaan?

A) Canaan was in the Promised Land

B) Canaan's sacrifice of children

C) Bestiality and other abominations

D) All of the above

139. Which river did the Israelites cross to enter Canaan?

A) Euphrates River

B) Nile River

C) Jordan River

D) Tigris River

140. Which prophet confronted King Ahab?

A) Elisha

B) Elijah

C) Isaiah

D) Hosea

141. Who was known as "a man after God's own heart" in Israel?

A) Saul

B) Solomon

C) Samuel

D) David

142. Who brought the Ark of the Covenant to Jerusalem?

A) Solomon

B) Saul

C) David

D) Jerusalem

143. Which tribe served as priests in Israel?

A) Levi

B) Judah

C) Benjamin

D) Dan

144. Who was the mother of Israelite prophet Samuel?

A) Sarah

B) Hannah

C) Rachel

D) Miriam

145. What did the Israelites worship when Moses was on Mount Sinai?

A) Bronze snake

B) Wooden idol

C) Stone statue

D) Golden calf

146. The heads of the tribes of Israel were the sons of which patriarch?

A) Abraham

B) Isaac

C) Jacob

D) Joseph

147. Which judge had his strength in his hair?

A) Samson

B) Gideon

C) Othniel

D) Jephthah

148. What festival commemorates the Israelites' escape from Egypt?

A) Passover

B) Pentecost

C) Yom Kippur

D) Hanukkah

149. Who was Israel's wisest king?

A) Saul

B) David

C) Solomon

D) Josiah

150. What did the Israelites carry that symbolized God's presence? Where was it?

A) A burning bush; in Paran

B) An image; in the Promised Land

C) The Ten Commandments; Mt. Sinai

D) Ark of the Covenant; the Tabernacle

151. *What was Israel's punishment for disbelief and rebellion in the wilderness?*

A) Defeat in battle

B) Wandering for 40 years

C) Famine

D) Disease

152. *Why did Israel fall?*

A) They ran out of resources

B) They sinned, and thus fell to Babylon

C) They became unproductive

D) They sinned, thus fell to the Assyrians

153. *Why did only the kids of the Israelites led by Moses enter the Promised Land?*

A) Parents wanted to go back to Egypt

B) Parents didn't know where it was

C) Parents enjoyed the wilderness

D) Parents were ill

ANSWERS

124. D)	125. A)	126. C)
127. B)	128. B)	129. A)
130. C)	131. A)	132. D)
133. A)	134. B)	135. C)
136. D)	137. A)	138. D)
139. C)	140. B)	141. D)
142. C)	143. A)	144. B)
145. D)	146. C)	147. A)
148. A)	149. C)	150. D)
151. B)	152. D)	153. A)

A solid match.

WOMEN OF THE BIBLE

30 QUESTIONS

*Favour is deceitful, and
beauty is vain: But a woman
that feareth the LORD,
she shall be praised.*
Proverbs 31:30

154. Who was known for being a judge in Israel?

A) Jael

B) Deborah

C) Miriam

D) Hannah

155. Who was the wife of Isaac?

A) Leah

B) Rebekah

C) Rachel

D) Zilpah

156. Which woman turned into a pillar of salt?

A) Lot's wife

B) Sarah

C) Eve

D) Rebekah

157. Who helped the Israelite spies in Jericho?

A) Miriam

B) Deborah

C) Rahab

D) Hagar

158. Who tested Solomon's knowledge with questions and riddles?

A) Esther

B) Bathsheba

C) Queen of Sheba

D) Jezebel

159. Which woman betrayed Samson?

A) Ruth

B) Delilah

C) Miriam

D) Tamar

160. Who anointed David as king?

A) Abigail

B) Deborah

C) Nathan's mother

D) Hannah

161. Which queen refused to appear before King Xerxes?

A) Vashti

B) Esther

C) Bathsheba

D) Abigail

162. Who told the Virgin Mary "Blessed art thou among women?"

A) Delilah

B) Sarah

C) Elizabeth

D) Leah

163. *Who was the wife of Jacob, mother of Joseph?*

A) Leah

B) Rachel

C) Bilhah

D) Zilpah

164. *Who was the only female ruler of Judah?*

A) Bathsheba

B) Jezebel

C) Michal

D) Athaliah

165. *Which three women are ancestors of Jesus?*

A) Tamar, Ruth and Rahab

B) Tamar, Rahab and Athaliah

C) Ruth, Rahab and Hannah

D) Ruth, Rahab and Queen of Sheba

166. Who is known as the Blessed Virgin?

A) Athaliah

B) Mary Magdalene

C) Mary, mother of Jesus

D) Elizabeth

167. Who is known for hiding her son, Moses, in a basket?

A) Miriam

B) Jochebed

C) Zipporah

D) Rahab

168. Which woman was known for being the Jewish wife of a Persian king?

A) Ruth

B) Abigail

C) Esther

D) Naomi

169. *What was the name of David's daughter who was violated by her brother Amnon?*

A) Salome

B) Michal

C) Abishag

D) Tamar

170. *Who was the first person to see the risen Jesus?*

A) Mary Magdalene

B) Mary, mother of Jesus

C) Mary of Cleophas

D) Mary of Bethany

171. *Who was the mother of John the Baptist?*

A) Elizabeth

B) Margaret

C) Martha

D) Anna

172. Who was the wife of Abraham?

A) Hagar

B) Sarah

C) Rebekah

D) Leah

173. Which wife of King David was known for giving him advice?

A) Michal

B) Abigail

C) Bathsheba

D) Tamar

174. Who was the servant of Sarah who bore Abraham's first son?

A) Rebekah

B) Leah

C) Hagar

D) Zilpah

175. Who was the sister of Lazarus and Mary, known for her hospitality?

A) Miriam

B) Deborah

C) Esther

D) Martha

176. Which woman was known for her loyalty to Naomi?

A) Orpah

B) Hagar

C) Michal

D) Ruth

177. Who was the wicked queen of Israel?

A) Athaliah

B) Bathsheba

C) Jezebel

D) Esther

178. Who was the wife of Jacob who had a son named Benjamin?

A) Leah

B) Rachel

C) Zilpah

D) Bilhah

179. Who saved her people from destruction by revealing her identity to a king?

A) Esther

B) Ruth

C) Abigail

D) Deborah

180. Who was the mother of King Solomon?

A) Michal

B) Bathsheba

C) Esther

D) Abigail

181. Who was the woman who killed Sisera by driving a tent peg through his head?

A) Delilah

B) Hagar

C) Miriam

D) Jael

182. Who was the wife of King Saul who loved David?

A) Abigail

B) Esther

C) Michal

D) Hagar

183. Which woman is the first person to name God in the Bible? What name was used?

A) Deborah; *Immanuel* (God is with us.)

B) Ruth; *Yeshua* (Deliverance)

C) Naomi; *Elijah* (Yahweh is my God.)

D) Hagar; *El Roi* (The God who sees me.)

ANSWERS

154. B)	155. B)	156. A)
157. C)	158. C)	159. B)
160. D)	161. A)	162. C)
163. B)	164. D)	165. A)
166. C)	167. B)	168. C)
169. D)	170. A)	171. A)
172. B)	173. B)	174. C)
175. D)	176. D)	177. C)
178. B)	179. A)	180. B)
181. D)	182. C)	183. D)

Great work!

GOD'S COVENANTS

12 QUESTIONS

*My covenant will I not
break, nor alter the thing that
is gone out of my lips.*
Psalm 89:34

184. What is the purpose of God's covenants?

A) To create nations

B) To set boundaries

C) To establish relationships

D) To set laws for humans

185. What is another word for covenant?

A) Condition

B) Law

C) Boundary

D) Promise

186. What sign did God give Noah as a covenant?

A) Rainbow

B) Dove

C) Fire

D) Stone tablets

187. What did God promise Abraham?

A) Wealth

B) Land and descendants

C) Victory in battles

D) Long life

188. How many major covenants are in the Bible?

A) 8-12

B) 3

C) 5-7

D) 10

189. Which covenant gave laws to Israel?

A) Davidic Covenant

B) Mosaic Covenant

C) Abrahamic Covenant

D) New Covenant

190. *What event fulfilled the New Covenant?*

A) Jesus' birth and crucifixion

B) Jesus' baptism and preaching

C) Jesus' death and resurrection

D) Jesus' ascension into Heaven

191. *What was the sign of the Abrahamic covenant?*

A) Rainbow

B) Circumcision

C) Sacrifice

D) Prayer

192. *Which book details God's covenant with David?*

A) Genesis

B) Psalms

C) Isaiah

D) 2 Samuel

193. What did God say in His Davidic Covenant?

A) David will have many descendants

B) David's kingdom will last forever

C) David will live a long life

D) David would defeat Goliath

194. The covenant of works was made with

A) Amos before Israel fell.

B) Abraham before Isaac was born.

C) Adam and Eve before the fall.

D) John before Jesus was born.

195. The New Covenant is between God and

A) Jesus.

B) humans.

C) Mary.

D) the children of Israel.

ANSWERS

184. C)	185. D)	186. A)
187. A)	188. C)	189. B)
190. C)	191. B)	192. D)
193. B)	194. C)	195. B)

Knocked it out of the park.

SALVATION IN THE BIBLE

18 QUESTIONS

*Neither is there salvation in
any other: for there is none
other name under heaven
given among men, whereby
we must be saved.*
Acts 4:12

196. What is salvation?

A) A state of happiness

B) Deliverance from sin

C) Rescued from mistakes

D) The afterlife

197. Which verse talks about salvation?

A) Acts 20:35

B) Deuteronomy 28:11

C) Job 1:21

D) Ephesians 2:8

198. What does Romans 3:23 say all have done?

A) Sinned

B) Obeyed

C) Worked

D) Prayed

199. What does repentance lead to?

A) Happiness

B) Power

C) Salvation

D) Wealth

200. Who needs salvation according to the Bible?

A) Only sinners

B) Everyone

C) The righteous

D) Angels

201. What does Romans 10:9 say one must do to be saved?

A) Confess and believe

B) Fast and be humble

C) Work hard

D) Read the Bible

202. *What does one receive after salvation?*

A) Power

B) Riches

C) Honor

D) Eternal life

203. *Who fell out of a window while Paul was preaching and was saved from death?*

A) Timothy

B) Eutychus

C) Silas

D) Barnabas

204. *What is the role of Jesus in salvation?*

A) Teacher

B) Warrior

C) Redeemer

D) Prophet

205. Which book speaks of salvation through a new covenant?

A) Jeremiah

B) Exodus

C) Job

D) Proverbs

206. Who said "Salvation belongs to our God"?

A) Moses

B) John

C) David

D) Angels

207. Which of Jesus' parables teaches about lost salvation?

A) The Good Samaritan

B) The Prodigal Son

C) The Sower

D) The Lost Coin

208. *What must one be "born of" to enter the kingdom?*

A) Fire and faith

B) Blood and soil

C) Spirit and water

D) Soil and God

209. *What symbolizes salvation in Exodus?*

A) Manna

B) The Red Sea

C) The Ark

D) The Tabernacle

210. *What is salvation compared to in Isaiah 12:3?*

A) Gold

B) Oil

C) Wine

D) Water

211. Who were saved from being burned in a furnace for their faithfulness to God?

A) Daniel and Shadrach

B) Mesach, Saul, and Daniel

C) Shadrach, Mesach, and Abednego

D) Mesach, Abrach, and Domingo

212. Who did Jesus save by rising them from the dead?

A) Jairus' daughter

B) Lazarus

C) Widow of Nain's son

D) All of the above

213. Who did Jesus save from being stoned?

A) An adulterous woman

B) A prostitute

C) A Samaritan woman

D) Mary Magdalene

ANSWERS

196. B)	197. D)	198. A)
199. C)	200. B)	201. A)
202. D)	203. B)	204. C)
205. A)	206. D)	207. B)
208. C)	209. B)	210. D)
211. C)	212. B)	213. A)

Favored, aren't ya?

BIBLICAL PLACES

30 QUESTIONS

*Can any hide himself in secret
places that I shall not see
him? saith the Lord. Do not
I fill heaven and earth?
saith the Lord.*

Jeremiah 23:24

214. Where did Moses receive the Ten Commandments?

A) Mount Carmel

B) Mount Horeb

C) Mount Ararat

D) Mount Sinai

215. Where did Jesus perform His first miracle?

A) Cana

B) Jerusalem

C) Nazareth

D) Bethany

216. Where was the Apostle Paul born?

A) Tarsus

B) Corinth

C) Ephesus

D) Antioch

217. Where did Jonah go after fleeing God's command?

A) Nineveh

B) Joppa

C) Tarshish

D) Babylon

218. Where was Jesus crucified?

A) Bethlehem

B) Golgotha

C) Nazareth

D) Jerusalem

219. What was the capital of Israel?

A) Bethel

B) Jerusalem

C) Samariah

D) Galilee

220. Where was the Tower of Babel built?

A) Persia

B) Jerusalem

C) Nineveh

D) Babylon

221. Where did Elijah challenge the prophets of Baal?

A) Mount Carmel

B) Mount Sinai

C) Mount Zion

D) Bethel

222. Where did Jesus experience The Agony in the Garden before His crucifixion?

A) Garden of Gethsemane

B) Mount of Olives

C) Ives of Eden

D) Garden of Golgotha

223. Where did David defeat Goliath?

A) Jericho

B) Hebron

C) Valley of Elah

D) Bethlehem

224. Where was Paul imprisoned?

A) Ephesus

B) Rome

C) Antioch

D) Corinth

225. To where did Mary and Joseph escape to hide baby Jesus from King Herod?

A) Assyria

B) Jordan

C) Turkey

D) Egypt

226. Where did God part the waters for the Israelites led by Moses?

A) Jordan River

B) Sea of Galilee

C) Red Sea

D) Nile River

227. Where did Jesus meet the Samaritan woman?

A) Samaria

B) Jacob's Well

C) Jerusalem

D) Nazareth

228. Where did Lot and his family flee from?

A) Nineveh

B) Sodom

C) Babylon

D) Gomorrah

229. Where did God speak to Moses through the burning bush?

A) Mount Sinai

B) Mount Horeb

C) Mount Ararat

D) Mount Carmel

230. Where did the walls fall after Joshua's march?

A) Jericho

B) Hebron

C) Ai

D) Bethel

231. Where did Ruth meet Boaz?

A) Jerusalem

B) Bethel

C) Moab

D) Bethlehem

232. *To where was Joseph sold by his brothers?*

A) Hebron

B) Dothan

C) Shechem

D) Egypt

233. *Where did the transfiguration of Jesus happen?*

A) Mount of Olives

B) Mount Sinai

C) Mount Tabor

D) Mount Carmel

234. *Where was the temple built by Solomon?*

A) Shiloh

B) Hebron

C) Jerusalem

D) Bethel

235. Where did Jesus calm the storm?

A) Dead Sea

B) Red Sea

C) Sea of Galilee

D) Jordan River

236. Where did Samson push down the pillars?

A) Ashdod

B) Gaza

C) Bethel

D) Jericho

237. Where did Daniel face the lions?

A) Jerusalem

B) Persia

C) Nineveh

D) Babylon

238. To where did Elijah go in a whirlwind?

A) Heaven

B) Sinai

C) Mount Carmel

D) Jordan

239. To where was John the Apostle exiled?

A) Cyprus

B) Malta

C) Crete

D) Patmos

240. From where did Jesus ascend to heaven?

A) Mount Tabor

B) Mount Carmel

C) Mount of Olives

D) Mount Sinai

241. What was the capital of Judah?

A) Bethlehem

B) Capernaum

C) Bethel

D) Nazareth

242. Where did Jesus turn water into wine?

A) At a wedding in Cana, Galilee

B) At a baptism in Jericho, Canaan

C) At a funeral in Bethlehem, Israel

D) At a baptism in Nazareth, Israel

243. What are three cities Paul traveled to and wrote New Testament letters to?

A) Corcyra, Corinth and Athens

B) Philippi, Corinth and Thessaloniki

C) Athens, Neapoli and Patras

D) Thessaloniki, Ephesus, and Patras

ANSWERS

214. D)	215. A)	216. A)
217. C)	218. B)	219. C)
220. D)	221. A)	222. A)
223. C)	224. B)	225. D)
226. C)	227. B)	228. B)
229. B)	230. A)	231. D)
232. D)	233. C)	234. C)
235. C)	236. B)	237. D)
238. A)	239. D)	240. C)
241. A)	242. A)	243. B)

Nicely done!

BIBLICAL CHARACTERS

30 QUESTIONS

Male and female created
He them; and blessed them,
and called their name
Adam, in the day when
they were created.
Genesis 5:2

244. What was the name of the man with the talking donkey?

A) Barth

B) Balaam

C) Bethel

D) Baalah

245. What was Goliath?

A) An Ammonite

B) An Israelite

C) A Philistine

D) A Canaanite

246. Who was Adam and Eve's grandson?

A) Enoch

B) Abraham

C) Noah

D) Cain

247. Who interpreted Pharaoh's dreams?

A) Daniel

B) Aaron

C) Moses

D) Joseph

248. Whose staff turned into a snake?

A) John

B) Aaron

C) Peter

D) Elijah

249. Who were the mysterious, giant beings mentioned in the Old Testament?

A) The Philistines

B) The Cherubim

C) The Seraphim

D) The Nephilim

250. Who was the first judge of Israel?

A) Jephthah

B) Deborah

C) Samson

D) Othniel

251. Who lost his children, his money, and his health but refused to curse God?

A) Hosea

B) Josiah

C) Job

D) Bildad

252. Which angel told Mary that she was chosen to be the mother of Jesus?

A) Michael

B) Daniel

C) Raphael

D) Gabriel

253. Who was Moses' father-in-law?

A) Jethro

B) Saul

C) David

D) Samuel

254. Who was taken into Heaven in a fiery chariot?

A) The Prophet Elijah

B) The Prophet Elisha

C) The Prophet Hosea

D) The Prophet Josiah

255. Who was thrown into the lions' den?

A) Daniel

B) Jeremiah

C) Elijah

D) Joseph

256. What did the three wise men bring baby Jesus?

A) gold, sage and myrrh

B) silver, frankincense and myrrh

C) silver, sage and frankincense

D) gold, frankincense and myrrh

257. Who was King Solomon's son?

A) King Saul

B) King Rehoboam

C) King David

D) King Samuel

258. Which King of Ethiopia (Cush) is mentioned in the Bible?

A) King Ahaz

B) King Herod

C) King Taharqa (Tirhaka)

D) King Solomon

259. Who lead the Israelites across the Jordan River after God parted the waters?

A) Moses

B) Joshua

C) Elisha

D) Ahab

260. Which sons were swallowed by the Earth as God's punishment?

A) The sons of Levi

B) The Sons of Eli

C) The Sons of Baal

D) The Sons of Korah

261. What was Abraham's previous name?

A) Adam

B) Isaac

C) Abram

D) Ibrahl

262. Who was Ruth's mother-in-law?

A) Rachel

B) Naomi

C) Deborah

D) Esther

263. Who was the tax collector turned disciple?

A) John

B) Matthew

C) Peter

D) Andrew

264. Who got cured of his blindness by Anaias and Jesus?

A) Samson

B) Bethel

C) Paul

D) Daniel

265. Who was the first ever martyr in Christianity?

A) Peter

B) James

C) Stephen

D) Paul

266. Who was Moses' wife?

A) Zipporah

B) Miriam

C) Beth

D) Caliphia

267. Who saw the burning bush?

A) Elijah

B) Moses

C) Joshua

D) Abraham

268. Who was Isaac's wife?

A) Leah

B) Rachel

C) Sarah

D) Rebekah

269. Who was the prophet during King Ahab's reign?

A) Isaiah

B) Elijah

C) Amos

D) Elisha

270. What did Israelites do to be spared from the tenth plague or angel of death in Egypt?

A) Marked their door with lamb's blood

B) Sacrificed a goat

C) Marked their clothes with myrr

D) Hummed a protective hymn

271. Who was Esther's cousin?

A) Nehemiah

B) Mordecai

C) Haman

D) Ezra

272. Who was Jacob's first wife?

A) Leah

B) Rachel

C) Sarah

D) Rebekah

273. Who interpreted King Nebuchadnezzar's dream?

A) Jeremiah

B) Isaiah

C) Daniel

D) Joseph

ANSWERS

244. B)	245. C)	246. A)
247. D)	248. B)	249. D)
250. D)	251. C)	252. D)
253. A)	254. A)	255. A)
256. D)	257. B)	258. C)
259. B)	260. D)	261. C)
262. B)	263. B)	264. C)
265. C)	266. A)	267. B)
268. D)	269. B)	270. A)
271. B)	272. A)	273. C)

The Lord would be proud.

THE BIBLE

30 QUESTIONS

Every word of God is pure:
He is a shield unto them that
put their trust in Him.
Proverbs 30:5

274. How many books are in the Bible?

A) 39

B) 54

C) 72

D) 66

275. How many books are in the Old Testament?

A) 27

B) 39

C) 46

D) 33

276. How many books are in the New Testament?

A) 27

B) 22

C) 34

D) 29

277. What are the first five books of the Bible called?

   A) The Scrolls

   B) The Apocrypha

   C) The Torah

   D) The Talmud

278. What is the last book of the Bible?

   A) Jude

   B) Revelation

   C) Malachi

   D) John

279. Which book has the longest chapter?

   A) Isaiah

   B) Psalms

   C) Genesis

   D) Jeremiah

280. What is the shortest book in the Bible?

A) 3 John

B) 2 John

C) Mark

D) Titus

281. What is the longest book in the Bible?

A) Jeremiah

B) Genesis

C) Isaiah

D) Psalms

282. How many Gospels are in the New Testament?

A) 3

B) 4

C) 5

D) 2

283. How many prophecies about Jesus came true in the Bible?

A) 50+

B) 120+

C) 300+

D) 200+

284. What genre is the Book of Psalms?

A) History

B) Poetry

C) Prophecy

D) Law

285. Which Bible verse is the shortest?

A) 1 Thessalonians 5:16

B) John 11:35

C) Genesis 1:1

D) Luke 17:32

286. *Who is traditionally credited with writing the first five books of the Bible?*

A) Samuel

B) Joshua

C) David

D) Moses

287. *Which book is known for its wisdom literature?*

A) Job

B) Proverbs

C) Ecclesiastes

D) All of the above

288. *What language was most of the Old Testament originally written in?*

A) Hebrew

B) Latin

C) Aramaic

D) Greek

289. What language was most of the New Testament originally written in?

A) Hebrew

B) Latin

C) Greek

D) Aramaic

290. What is the overall storyline of the Bible?

A) Man cannot escape sin and death

B) Man's sins are then redeemed by Jesus

C) Heaven and Earth will be reunited

D) All of the above

291. What is the only book of the Bible that doesn't directly mention God's name?

A) 2 Kings

B) Esther

C) 1 Chronicles

D) Ecclesiastes

292. *When were chapters and verses added to the Bible?*

A) in the 1900s

B) in the 300s

C) in the 1200s

D) in the 1700s

293. *Which book features the story of David and Goliath?*

A) 1 Samuel

B) 2 Samuel

C) 1 Kings

D) Judges

294. *How many songs are in the Bible?*

A) 120+

B) 40+

C) 350+

D) 185+

295. Who wrote the most words in the New Testament?

A) Matthew

B) Luke

C) John

D) James

296. Over how many years was the Bible written?

A) 1500+

B) 800+

C) 2000+

D) 300+

297. Which book contains the Beatitudes?

A) John

B) Matthew

C) Luke

D) Mark

298. What type of book is Revelation?

A) History

B) Epistle

C) Poetry

D) Prophecy

299. Who are the two most mentioned people in the Bible?

A) Paul and then Jesus

B) Jesus and then Paul

C) Jesus and then David

D) Jesus and then Moses

300. What has more manuscripts than any other document from the Ancient World?

A) The Torah

B) The New Testament

C) The Old Testament

D) All of the above

301. Where do the words "the Bible" come from?

A) Greek: "ta biblia" (the books)

B) Latin: "biblia sacra" (holy book)

C) Hebrew: "Tanakh" (Bible)

D) Aramaic: "Targum" (Bible)

302. Which are true of the Bible?

A) Best-selling book globally

B) Most stolen book globally

C) Over 600k words total

D) All of the above

303. How many authors are believed to have contributed to the Bible?

A) About 10

B) About 25

C) About 40

D) About 50

ANSWERS

274. D)	**275. B)**	**276. A)**
277. C)	**278. B)**	**279. B)**
280. A)	**281. A)**	**282. B)**
283. C)	**284. B)**	**285. B)**
286. D)	**287. D)**	**288. A)**
289. C)	**290. D)**	**291. B)**
292. C)	**293. A)**	**294. D)**
295. B)	**296. A)**	**297. B)**
298. D)	**299. C)**	**300. B)**
301. A)	**302. D)**	**303. C)**

Well played!

Enjoyed this book? Scan the QR code to get this complimentary fun, <u>free</u> *He Is Risen trivia game* (left), or this **Bible trivia games bundle** (right):

He Is Risen Trivia Game

Bible Trivia Games BUNDLE

Need **fun**, **educational** Bible games for Sunday school, adult ministry, homeschool, events, church picnics, or youth group? Find them at *Bon Roi Press:* **$2.99** each, or **$4.99** per bundle!

Trinity BUNDLE

Summer-Themed

Lost Sheep Group Game

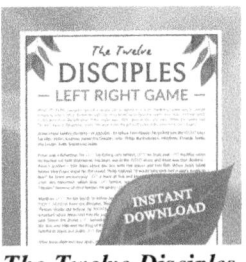

The Twelve Disciples

Jonah and the Whale

Parables BUNDLE

Beatitudes Crossword

Bible Back to School

Women of the Bible

Holy Spirit Group Game

Bon Roi Press

Browse Etsy Shop

Browse TPT Store